A POWER HIGHER

THE DOCTRINE OF THE FULLNESS OF THE HOLY SPIRIT

BY

E. A. JOHNSTON

OTHER BOOKS

BY

Dr. E. A. JOHNSTON

Many of the following books may be purchased individually or as a set by going to Dr. Johnston's webpage in the bookstore at The Old Paths Publications that has links to distributors. Go to:

www.theoldpathspublications.com/Pages/Authors/Johnston.htm

1. *"A Heart Awake: The Authorized Biography of J. Sidlow Baxter"* Foreword by Adrian Rogers (The Old Paths Publications, www.theoldpathspublications.com).
2. *"Realities Of Revival"* Foreword by Stephen F. Olford (Gospel Folio Press, Canada; 2005).
3. *"Revival Trilogy"* (The Old Paths Publications: www.theoldpathspublications.com).
4. *"The Man God Uses"* (The Old Paths Publications: www.theoldpathspublications.com).
5. *"Recovery of the Gospel"* (The Old Paths Publications: www.theoldpathspublications.com).
6. *"Ten Alarming Sermons"* (The Old Paths Publications: www.theoldpathspublications.com).
7. *"How to Have a Daily Quiet Time"* (The Old Paths Publications: www.theoldpathspublications.com).

8. *"Faith Lessons in a Dynamite God"* (The Old Paths Publications: www.theoldpathspublications.com).

9. *Sayings of E.A. Johnston Hope For Hurting Hearts"* (The Old Paths Publications: www.theoldpathspublications.com).

10. *"Call To Revival"* Foreword By Colin Peckham (Gospel Folio Press, Canada; 2008).

11. *"The Church In Revival"* Foreword By Richard Owen Roberts (Gospel Folio Press, Canada; 2008).

12. *"Olford On Scroggie: Stephen Olford's Notes on the Sermon Outlines of Graham Scroggie"* Co-authored with Stephen Olford (The Old Paths Publications: www.theoldpathspublications.com).

13. *"George Whitefield A Definitive Biography, Volumes 1 and 2 Combined"* (The Old Paths Publications: www.theoldpathspublications.com).

14. *"George Whitefield A Definitive Biography In Two Volumes"* (American edition published by Revival Literature, Asheville; 2012).

15. *"God's Hitchhike Evangelist The Biography Of Rolfe Barnard"* Foreword By Bob Doom (The Old Paths Publications: www.theoldpathspublications.com).

16. *"Asahel Nettleton Revival Preacher"* Foreword By John Thornbury, Preface By Richard Owen Roberts (The Old Paths Publications: www.theoldpathspublications.com).

17. *"Sermons For Revival"* (The Old Paths Publications: www.theoldpathspublications.com).

18. *"A Noble Company Biographical Essays on Notable Particular Baptists in America Volume 11: Portrait of Rolfe Barnard"* (Particular Baptist Press, Springfield; 2018).

19. *"Lectures On Revival For A Laodicean Church,"* (The Old Paths Publications: www.theoldpathspublications.com)

20. *"Sam Jones, A New Biography"* (The Old Paths Publications: www.theoldpathspublications.com)

21. E. A. Johnston's Book Set, (The Old Paths Publications, www.theoldpathspublications.com (30% off retail)

Many of these books can be purchased in The Old Paths Publications Bookstore at a discounted price. Go here:

E. A. Johnston Books

(https://www.theoldpathspublications.com/Pages/Authors/Johnston.htm)

or

https://www.theoldpathspublications.com/Pages/BookStore.htm

DEDICATION

The following chapters on the doctrine of the Fullness of the Holy Spirt are hereby dedicated to the memory of my homiletical mentor, colleague, and friend, Dr. Stephen F. Olford who taught me by his example that the anointing of the Holy Spirit is available to any serious Christian who desires and is willing to appropriate that power for ministry and service today

Dr. Steven Olford (L) and Dr. E.A. Johnston

8

TABLE OF CONTENTS

INTRODUCTION

Is there a legitimate reason why most Christians in America are not persecuted for their faith? Could it be that they blend in too well with pagan society to where there is little noticeable difference? Is there a reason why the church in America, for the most part, lacks authority and power? The dissimilarities of the early church as depicted in the Book of Acts and the modern church today are startling. The early Christians had power and authority attending their witness and their worship for Christ and the Gospel. They were physically dragged from their homes and loved ones and beaten for their testimony in Christ Jesus. Those early believers who refused to say, "Caesar is Lord" and who boldly proclaimed, "Jesus is Lord" were tied to posts in Nero's Circus and doused with oil to be human torches to light the evening chariot races. Those earnest believers who refused to compromise with the pagan society around them were fed to wild beasts in the Colosseum and torn asunder for their testimony in Christ Jesus.

I first encountered the modern disbelief in the power of the Holy Spirit for our day, when I was taking my oral exam for my Ph.D., and I mentioned to one of the two seminary professors who were conducting my oral exam, that there was a vast difference between the Christianity of our day as compared to the early days of the church, as seen in the Book of Acts. And my seminary professor reprimanded me and said, "That was for then, and not for now." If the professor wants to live a powerless life for Christ, then it's up to him, but I hungered for MORE. I wanted to have the same power and authority that the early church possessed and I believe there is biblical evidence to back up the fact that the Holy Spirit did not go out of business once the early church was established.

If that "power higher" was reserved only for the Apostles and early church then how does one explain the mighty evangelistic ministry of a George Whitefield? How did Whitefield gather crowds at 5am to stand in the cold and rain for two hours to hear him preach the glorious Gospel of the Son of God? Why was George Whitefield persecuted so? Often while he preached in the open air he had pieces of dead cats thrown at him and he was pelted with stones. One time while preaching to a mob in Ireland he was stoned and almost killed. While on his second journey in America he was introduced to a minister from

Ireland, who upon greeting him, Whitefield bowed and removed his beaver cap while pointing to a large scar on his forehead with the comment, "This Sir, is the wound I received for preaching Christ in your country."

If the power of the Holy Spirit was only reserved for the early church then how does one explain a D. L. Moody who was an uneducated man who after his baptism of the Holy Ghost was able to hold ten thousand hearers at a time for weeks at a time in major metropolises of Glasgow, Edinburgh, and London? How does one explain a Charles Finney? Or a Mordecai Ham? Or a Sam Jones? Each of these men had the authority of the Holy Spirit upon them in power when they preached and revival followed. Go study the life of the Chinese evangelist, John Sung, who shook China for God with signs and wonders between the two World Wars. Over three hundred thousand souls were saved under Sung's mighty ministry and there were many instances of cripples being healed, the deaf regaining their hearing and the blind receiving their sight!

I submit to you friends, that the power of the Holy Spirit that attended the ministries of John Wesley and George Whitefield, and Finney and

Moody and Mordecai Ham and Sam Jones is still available to us today IF WE KNOW HOW TO APPROPRIATE HIM. This book will walk you through the doctrine of the Fullness of the Holy Spirit which will give power in the pulpit and consistency in the walk with God. Much of what I lay out in this book I learned at the feet of my homiletical mentor, Dr. Stephen F. Olford who taught me the doctrine of the FULLNESS OF THE SPIRIT in the same way he taught it personally to a young Billy Graham.

CHAPTER ONE: MISSING DOCTRINES AND REVIVAL

"Give me one hundred men who fear nothing but God, and hate nothing but sin, and I will shake the gates of hell."

John Wesley

If one studies the history of revival one will find that often a spiritual awakening began when a lost doctrine was recovered and preached prominently once more. This was the case with a Catholic monk, Martin Luther, who discovered the lost doctrine of justification by faith in his day and it transformed his life as he began to proclaim it (amidst persecution) and spearheaded a Reformation!

This was the case with a young George Whitefield who discovered the missing doctrine of regeneration in his day by reading the book by the Scotsman, Henry Scougal "The Life of God in the Soul of Man" and it transformed his life and he went forward with the main message of "Ye must be Born Again" shaking two continents for God in revival!

This was the case with Charles Finney and Asahel Nettleton the two main leaders of the Second Great Awakening, who both preached in their day the missing doctrine of repentance and stirred a nation for God and the Gospel!

Such was the case of D. L. Moody who laid hold of the lost doctrine of the Love of God as he heard it from the lips of the little Englishman, Henry Moorehouse, and Moody went on to shake entire cities with that message of God's love toward sinners!

Mordecai Ham turned entire cities upside down with the Gospel using the missing doctrine in his day of The Lordship of Jesus Christ. "I preached the absolute Lordship of Jesus Christ. I allowed for no compromise, but hammered this one thought that Christ Jesus must have first place, first call, and first allegiance. I made that the keynote of all my meetings."[1]

---

[1] Edward Ham, "Fifty Years On The Battle Front With Christ. A Biography of Mordecai F. Ham", (Louisville: The Old Kentucky Home Revivalist, 1959), p 119.

In our day, the missing doctrine of The Fullness of the Holy Spirit if taught, grasped, appropriated, and proclaimed could bring a spiritual awakening to a sin sick society and ignite a slumbering church! Missing doctrines recovered and proclaimed can be the seedbed for revival and can effect change!

18

CHAPTER TWO:
DR. STEPHEN F. OLFORD

"The Word of God cannot be mastered until we are mastered by the Word of God."

Stephen F. Olford

Stephen F. Olford (March 29, 1918—August 29, 2004) was an evangelical leader who trained thousands of pastors in expository preaching at his pastor training center in Memphis, Tennessee. He was born in Africa of missionary parents and was a leading figure in Christianity. He began his pastoral ministry in 1953, by serving The Duke Street Baptist Church in Richmond Surrey, England. He then pastored the historic Calvary Baptist Church in New York City from 1959-1973. He is the author of several books and a renown international evangelist. He was most influential in the life of Billy Graham, in regard to teaching Graham the doctrine of "The Fullness of The Spirit". We see from the following account of Olford's testimony, "My Most Memorable Encounter With God":

"I was so caught up in the wonder of this encounter with God that I cut short my stay at Porthcawl by three days and returned to Newport to share the news! Later that week I spoke at a rally of young people in Cardiff. The large church was packed, and God moved in such power that I was there until midnight, dealing with seeking souls. There was an authority in preaching I had never known before.

"The next appointment was a week of meetings at the Hildenborough Hall Conference Center, near London, under the directorship of the British evangelist, Mr. Tom Rees. Each day, I spoke on prayer in the morning, and on the Holy Spirit in the evening, and the Lord was pleased to send us 'times of refreshing' from His presence.

"Friday night we gathered for a period of sharing, to be followed by a concluding message. American visitors were with us on that occasion. Among them was a young man by the name of Billy Graham. As he heard the testimonies of these young people who had entered into the fullness of the Holy Spirit, and then listened to my exposition of Ephesians 5:18, he walked up to me, at the close of the service, with that resolute look in his eyes and that determined thrust of his jaw, and asked to know more.

"We were unable to talk freely at the time, but made arrangements to meet in Wales. There I found that Billy was seeking for more of God with all his heart; and he felt that I could help him. For most of two days we were closeted at Pontypridd's hotel with our Bibles open, turning the pages as we studied passages and verses. The first day Billy learned more secrets of the 'quiet time.' The next, I expounded the fullness of the Holy Spirit in the life of a believer who is willing to bow daily and hourly to the sovereignty of Christ and to the authority of the Word. This lesson was so new to me that it cascaded out, revealing bright glimpses of the inexhaustible power of the love of God.

"Billy drank it in so avidly that I scarcely realized the heights and depths that his spiritual life had reached already. At the close of the second day we prayed, like Jacob of old laying hold of God, and crying, 'Lord, I will not let Thee go except Thou bless me,' until we came to a place of rest and rejoicing. And Billy Graham said, 'This is a turning point in my life, this will revolutionize my ministry.'"[2]

I first met Stephen Olford while he was conducting an institute on expository preaching at his training institute in Memphis, I was one of the students. On the third day there my entire life was turned upside down and the course of my life was altered from that point forward. I went in a secular business man; I came out a changed man who had a wide ministry before him both in writing and preaching.

Stephen Olford taught me how to preach and I was in the first graduating class of his school of preachers. He not only was my homiletical mentor, we co-authored a book together on his homiletical mentor, Dr. W. Graham Scroggie, entitled, *Olford on Scroggie* (see Old Paths Publications for copies). I eventually was asked to become a board member of Olford Ministries International. Dr. Olford taught me:

1. HOW TO HAVE A DAILY QUIET TIME
2. HOW TO BE AN EXPOSITORY PREACHER
3. HOW TO PREACH INCARNATIONALLY

---

[2] John Pollock, *Billy Graham: The Authorized Biography* (Minneapolis: Billy Graham Evangelistic Association), pp 38,39.

4. HOW TO BE ANOINTED WITH THE HOLY SPIRIT

5. HOW TO HAVE A CLEARER UNDERSTANING OF REVIVAL

So, the things I share with you in this little book are the things Stephen Olford taught me—and that is A LOT.

May God so use it in your own life friend is the prayer of my heart.

CHAPTER THREE: POWER IN THE PULPIT

"Quite suddenly, upon one and another came an overwhelming sense of the reality and awfulness of His presence and of eternal things."

Joseph Kemp, Pastor,
Charlotte Baptist Chapel, Edinburgh.

I have known men that when they preach they have POWER IN THE PULPIT. There is an obvious anointing of the Spirit of God upon them to where, as they proclaim the great doctrines of the Gospel, you are led to the very verge of eternity and confronted with the God of that eternity. This type of anointed preaching is the springboard for revival. What we have today, largely in our churches and standing behind our pulpits are TEACHERS and not PREACHERS. Men who use what academic training they have to teach a passage of Scripture to the best of their ability. Many of them, have to rely on funny stories and jokes to keep their audiences entertained, and these teachers hide behind laughter and entertainment because they know nothing of the power of God in a meeting!

On the other hand, read the following comments from Duncan Campbell, used mightily of God in revival on the Isle of Lewis, 1949-1952. Here is the testimony of a PREACHER full of the Holy Ghost:

> "The awful presence of God brought a wave of conviction of sin that caused even mature Christians to feel their sinfulness, bringing groans of distress and prayers of repentance from the unconverted. Strong men were bowed under the weight of sin and cries for mercy were mingled with shouts of joy from others who had passed into life."

Our churches in the land are under the remedial judgment of the WITHDRAWN PRESENCE OF GOD. Most men in ministry today are deeply unfamiliar with revival (as far as experiencing it) and unknowledgeable about it (as far as studying the history of revival). They are strangers to POWER IN THE PULPIT and lack the Spirit's anointing for such power. Listen to the words of Charles Finney in this regard:

> "I am afraid I must say, to the great majority of the ministers even of the present day, I think that their practical

views of preaching the Gospel, whatever their theological views may be, are very defective indeed; and that their want of unction, and of the power of the Holy Ghost is a radical defect in their preparation for the ministry."

Finney saw revival because Finney was full of the Holy Ghost as a preacher for revival! What we lack today are men who grasp this fundamental doctrine of the anointing for ministry and Christian service.

I have two earned doctorates, a British endorsed Ph.D., and a D.B.S. from two different seminaries. One day I was sitting in a preaching class with fellow students and the seminary professor was the Preaching Professor for this institution. He went on at length about how to be an effective communicator as a preacher, how to use illustrations in sermons, how to project one's voice in the pulpit, and how to use one's personality in the pulpit while preaching. And a student seated next to me raised his hand to ask a question. The young man said,

"I understand what you are saying to us on using our natural abilities to preach but when I study revival in history and see how Jonathan Edwards preached full of the Holy Ghost with an unction from on High and revival followed his preaching with power like that, it is quite the opposite of what you are teaching us."

The preaching professor looked at the student with disdain and in a condescending voice commented, "You, young man, are NO JONATHAN EDWARDS!"

Well, I believe that young man knew more about preaching than that egg-headed professor! And unfortunately, seminaries DO NOT TEACH YOU HOW TO PREACH. They teach you theology. They teach you hermeneutics and homiletics and how to project your voice and personality behind a pulpit but they leave out this whole aspect of POWER IN THE PULPIT which is only true preaching after all. Listen to what Dr. Martyn Llyod-Jones had to say on this very subject:

> "We all need to be reminded of this. Let me make a confession for all preachers. The outstanding temptation—the besetting sin—of every preacher, myself included, is that after

you have prepared your sermons you feel that all is well. You have your two sermons ready for Sunday. Well, that is all right. You have your notes, and you can speak, and you can deliver your message. But that is not preaching! That can be utterly useless. Oh, it may be entertaining, there may be a certain amount of intellectual stimulus and profit in that, but that is not preaching! Preaching is in demonstration of the Spirit and of power (1 Cor. 2:5). And a man has to realize, after he has prepared his sermons, that however perfectly he may have done so, that it is all waste and useless unless the power of the Spirit comes upon it and upon him. He must pray for that."[3]

What Dr. Stephen Olford taught me was not only a way of preaching but a way of living. Allow me to give you a description of him from a pastor in Dallas:

---

[3] Martyn Lloyd-Jones, *Revival* (Wheaton: Crossway Books, 1987), p 124.

Dr. Olford was invited to speak at a church in Dallas, Texas and the seminary intern of that church was asked by the pastor to go pick up Stephen Olford at the airport. The intern asked for a photo of Stephen Olford so he would recognize him when he saw him. The Pastor replied, "No need for that. Just go to the airport terminal and as the passengers deplane, look for a man WHO HAS GOD ALL OVER HIM." The seminary intern went to the airport terminal and looked at the arriving passengers, he noticed a man with a briefcase and his coat over his arm walking hurriedly to the gate and GOD WAS ALL OVER HIM. We read in 2 Kings 4:9:

> *"And she said unto her husband, Behold now, I perceive that is a holy man of God, which passeth by us continually."*

Allow me friends, to give you what I consider to be the perfect definition of Stephen Olford as a preacher full of the Holy Ghost. I was waiting for him in his study one day and in he came looking tired and haggard. He slumped into a chair (he was 86 at the time!) with the remark and following apology: "Pardon me Brother, pardon me, I must regather myself, I must regather myself. I have just finished preaching and VIRTUE HAS LEFT ME." Immediately, my mind ran to the passage of Scripture of the woman with the issue of blood who touched the hem of Jesus' garment:

> *"When she heard of Jesus, came in the press behind, and touched his garment. For she said, If I may touch but his clothes, I shall be whole. And straightway the fountain of her blood was dried up; and she felt in her body that she was healed of that plague. And Jesus, immediately knowing in himself that virtue had gone out of him, turned him about in the press, and said, Who touched my clothes?"*

That was the image that came to my mind as I sat next to Dr. Olford. That word "virtue" in the Greek is the word "Dunamis" which means POWER, and the word which we get our English word "Dynamite". Stephen Olford preached with power, with this virtue that Christ had, and when he preached he held a Bible in one hand and a stick of dynamite in the other! Stephen Olford was around 5'5 with his shoes on but when he entered the pulpit and expounded God's Word, he looked like a linebacker with the Chicago Bears! That is this

POWER IN THE PULPIT of which I speak friends. And this comes only by prayer and the appropriation of the FULLNESS OF THE HOLY SPIRIT.

One who understood this principle clearly was E. M. Bounds, pay attention to his words:

"What of unction? It is the indefinable in preaching which makes it preaching. It is that which distinguishes and separates preaching from all mere human addresses. It is the divine in preaching. It makes the preaching sharp to those who need sharpness. It distills as the dew to those who need to be refreshed.

"This unction comes to the preacher not in the study but in the closet. It is heaven's distillation in answer to prayer. It is the sweetest exhalation of the Holy Spirit. It impregnates, suffuses, softens, percolates, cuts, and soothes. It carries the Word like DYNAMITE (author's emphasis), like salt, like sugar; makes the Word a soother, an arraigner, a revealer, a searcher; makes the hearer a culprit or a saint, makes him weep like a child and live like a giant; opens his heart and his purse as gently, yet as strongly as the spring opens the leaves. This unction is not the gift of genius. It is not found in the halls of learning. No eloquence can woo it. No industry can win it. No prelatical hands can confer it. It is the gift of God—the signet set to his own messengers. It is heaven's knighthood given to the chosen true and brave ones who have sought this anointed honor through many an hour of tearful, wrestling prayer.

"Earnestness is good and impressive; genius is gifted and great. Thought kindles and inspires, but it takes a diviner endowment, a more powerful energy than earnestness or genius or thought to break the chains of sin, to win estranged and depraved hearts to God, to repair the breaches and restore the Church to her old ways of purity and power. Nothing but his holy unction can do this."[4]

In our next chapter we will go deeper into this power from on high.

---

[4] E. M. Bounds' *Preacher and Prayer, also included Never Quit Praying for Your Loved Ones* by Marion Price, Sr. (Asheville: Revival Literature, 2013), pp 69-70.

CHAPTER FOUR: CONSISTENCY IN THE LIFE

"Are we prepared to accept God's condemnation of our sinful flesh? To hesitate in our answer is to reveal that we have neither considered the sinlessness of the Savior or the sinfulness of our hearts. We must be prepared to accept the diagnosis of the divine Physician in order to experience the cure of victory."

Stephen F. Olford

The Christian life is an impossible life to live in the flesh—it cannot be done. There must be a higher power involved to experience any victory in our walk with God. For many believers, a life of inconsistency is the status quo. To many, the Christian life is like an elevator: one day you are on the top floor enjoying the view from the Penthouse Suite; and then, unexpectedly and unfathomably the next day you are down in the basement of defeat. This "up and down" existence for many Christians is all they know and they have gotten accustomed to what I term: "Elevator Christianity".

But there is a way to victory and consistency with God through His Holy Spirit and in His Word. When we examine our redemption in Christ Jesus we realize Jesus not only saves from the penalty of sin, but from the power of sin. Allow me to use the following illustration.

The ancient city of Ephesus (now modern Turkey) is where both the Apostle Paul and Apostle John lived and ministered there (though not at the same time). Some scholars believe the Gospel of John was written during John's time in Ephesus and tradition states he is buried in Ephesus beneath the ruins of the Church of St. John. The Apostle Paul lived in Ephesus for three years and he wrote 1 Corinthians there and probably Galatians. The main attraction in Ephesus was the temple of Diana (Artemis) and thousands of pilgrims each year came to worship at the temple which was responsible for much of the commerce to the city.

Years, ago I visited the excavated ruins of ancient Ephesus and I marveled as I took a guided tour among those well-preserved ruins. My local tour guide identified the various ruins and places we saw. And we came to a place called an "Agora", which was a marketplace, much like an outdoor shopping mall today. Items would be bought and sold in the Agora. Slaves were bought and sold in the Agora. One of the Greek words for "redemption" is the word, "agorazo" which means Jesus entered the marketplace of sin and purchased me with His blood. Christ saves me from the penalty of sin being my sin substitute. Another Greek word for "redemption" employs the preposition "ek" which means to "take out of." If you place the little Greek preposition "ek" in front of the word, "agorazo" you get the word for redemption, "ek-agorazo" which means: Christ not only entered the marketplace of sin and purchased me with His blood but He also brought me "up and out" of that marketplace of sin. Christ saves from the penalty of sin as well as the power of sin! Regarding our walk with God, our liberty in the Holy Spirit is not freedom to do what I want, but power to do what I ought. It is a power higher than my own ability. This is how I live the Christian life—by a power higher. To fully appropriate this "higher power" through the Spirit in us whereby the Holy Spirit is not merely resident—but President. And this comes through an encounter with God through a crises experience.

CHAPTER FIVE:
THE CRISIS EXPERIENCE

"Jacob may have been saved at Bethel, but he was conquered at Peniel."

E. A. Johnston

In the Book of Genesis is the record of Jacob's wrestling with the angel at the Brook Jabbok. He had gotten there with a sense of dread and utter dependance upon God for help and deliverance. News had come to him that his brother Esau (whom he had deceived and cheated) was coming to meet him, and not only that, "he cometh to meet thee, and four hundred men" (Genesis 32:6). This terrifying and alarming report completely unmanned and unnerved Jacob who was clearly outnumbered.

We read the account of Jacob's encounter with God in the following striking passage of Scripture:

"And he rose up that night, and took his two wives, and his two women-servants, and his eleven sons, and passed over the ford Jabbok. And he

took them, and sent them over the brook, and sent over that he had. And Jacob was left alone; and there wrestled a man with him until the breaking of the day. And when he saw that he prevailed not against him, he touched the hollow of his thigh; and the hollow of Jacob's thigh was out of joint, as he wrestled with him. and he said, "Let me go, for the day breaketh. And he said, I will not let thee go, except thou bless me. and he said unto him, What is thy name? and he said, Jacob. And he said, Thy name shall be called no more Jacob, but Israel: for as a prince hast thou power with God and with men, and hast prevailed. And Jacob asked him, and said, Tell me, I pray thee, thy name. And he said, Wherefore is it that thou dost ask after my name? And he blessed him there. And Jacob called the name of the place Peniel: for I have seen God face to face, and my life is preserved. And as he passed over Penuel the sun rose upon him, and he halted upon his thigh" (Genesis 32:22-31).

When the angel asked Jacob's name, he had to confess that he was a "supplanter", a cheat, a swindler. It was said of Jacob that he was so crooked he could hide behind a corkscrew! God straightened Jacob out at Jabbok in the shadow of Esau coming with four hundred men. Have we faced a crisis of our own "Personal Jabbok"? Have we been straightened out?

Have we come to the utter place of "Absolute Surrender" to God? Or have we merely given Him our partial surrender and not our whole heart? Jacob left Jabbok with a limp for the rest of his life from his wrestling with God; but he also learned how to lean on God for the rest of his life. Jacob went from being a self-reliant man to a God-dependent man. After this encounter with God at Peniel, Jacob had to use a staff, a walking stick, and with every step he took he winced in pain—as a reminder of his encounter with God, and with every step he took the self-life died a little more. Jacob finished his "up and down" life in Egypt, emerging at the very last upon the plane of triumphant faith and prophecy!

I had to come to this place in my own life. It was a pain-filled experience that did not occur in a few hours of prayer—but in a period of years.

Because I was such a "hard case" and "hard nut to crack" God had to take me through a deep well of heartache and heartbreak; tragedy and trial; adversity and affliction; correction and instruction; which transpired between deep valleys and high mountain peaks. Everyone is wired differently. You may have your "crisis" like Jacob and be done with it. Or, God, because of your stubbornness, may have to put you through His "Refiner's Fire". Either way, God will conquer you and make you more like Jesus if you are one of His children—because you are bought with a price and that price was His Blood!

Years ago, I woke up in the middle of the night and I thought I was having a heart attack. I had been working fourteen-hour days and getting up at 4:30am each morning to have my quiet time with the Lord. I was plumb worn out. I was carrying on a full time ministry and a full time secular career as a successful stockbroker. And as I sat there at 2am at my desk before my open Bible, I asked the Lord to come and get me and take me home—I was so exhausted I just wanted Heaven. I prayed and told Him, "I'm ready to come home now Lord. Will you come get me?" And He met me there in those early morning hours by speaking to my heart—not an audible voice but a Voice nonetheless. In the

Gospels Jesus usually answered a question with a question. That morning He answered my question with a question:

"What do you do for a living?"

"Investments," I answered.

"I have an investment in you and I will receive the dividends from my investment."

Case closed. I went back to bed. That was eighteen years ago and there have been a lot of dividends paid during that time. The whole point of a crisis with God is this: God gets serious with those who get serious with Him? Are you ready to get serious with Him? Are You?

CHAPTER SIX: EXAMPLES OF THREE MEN WHO HAD THIS POWER HIGHER

"God can only bless with the anointing of His Spirit those who pursue a life of holiness."

Stephen F. Olford

There is a passage in the Gospel of Luke whereby it states,

"And Jesus returned in the power of the Spirit into Galilee: and there went out a fame of him through all the region round about" (Luke 4:14).

There is a pattern for usefulness unto God and that is the fullness of the Holy Spirit or Second Blessing. Jesus was one hundred percent man and one hundred percent God but the humanity side of Jesus needed power from on High to do the Father's will while He was here on earth. There have been preachers whom I have known who have demonstrated this higher power from an anointing of the Holy Spirit. We get a sense of this from Luke's Gospel where John the Baptist makes the following startling statement: "John answered, saying unto them all, I indeed baptize you with water; but one mightier than I cometh, the latchet of whose shoes I am not worthy to unloose: he shall baptize you with the Holy Ghost and with fire" (Luke 3:16). The men in history whom God has used in mighty revivals had this "Holy Ghost fire"! George Whitefield had it. John Wesley had it. Jonathan Edwards had it. Finney had it. Moody had it. Sam Jones had it. And each of these men turned entire cities upside down with their ministries of Holy Ghost fire! The early church definitely had this fire! We read in Acts,

> *"But ye shall receive power, after that the Holy Ghost is come upon you: and ye shall be witnesses unto me both in Jerusalem, and in all Judea, and in Samaria, and unto the uttermost part of the earth"* (Acts 1:8).

When one studies historical revival certain truths emerge as they are unearthed in accentuating the common denominator in revival. It is always the manifest presence of God by His Spirit that brings awakening, conviction, and conversions.

It is no coincidence that the three most-used American evangelists of the 19th century each shared a common experience—an enduement of Holy Ghost power for service. It happened to Charles Finney, D. L. Moody, and Sam Jones. This was the secret to their power. And this anointing occurred to each of them BEFORE they were thrust onto a national stage of great usefulness.

It came to Dwight Lyman Moody in 1871, before he was greatly used of God in revival throughout Great Britain. It happened to Charles Grandison Finney before he was used of God in revivals during the Second Great Awakening. And it happened to Samuel Porter Jones before he was thrust into the national spotlight and so powerfully used in revivals throughout the whole of America. We will examine these men one by one and compare their unique yet common experience.

In 1871 D. L. Moody was hungering for something more for God.

> "An intense hunger and thirst for spiritual power was aroused in him by two women who used to attend the meetings and sit in the front seat. He could see by the expression on their faces that they were praying. At the

close of the service they would say to him: "'We have been praying for you.' "'Why don't you pray for the people?' Mr. Moody would ask. "'Because you need the power of the Spirit,' they would say. "There came a great hunger in my soul. I did not know what it was. I began to cry out as I never did before. I really felt that I did not want to live if I could not have this power for service."[5]

D. L. Moody would speak of his experience of 1871 in future sermons and considered it the watermark highlight of his effectiveness for Christ and the Gospel. Even near the end of his life in his last campaigns he would make mention of it.

"I was crying all the time that God would fill me with His Spirit. Well, one day, in the city of New York—oh, what a day!—I cannot describe it. I seldom refer to it; it is almost too sacred an experience to name. Paul had an experience of which he never spoke for

---

[5] William R. Moody, "The Life of Dwight L. Moody" (Chicago: Fleming Revell, 1900), pp146-147.

fourteen years. I can only say that God revealed Himself to me, and I had such an experience of His love that I had to ask Him to stay His Hand. I went to preaching again. The sermons were no different; I did not present any new truths, and yet hundreds were converted. I would not now be placed back where I was before that blessed experience if you should give me all the world—it would be as the small dust of the balance."[6]

Charles Finney had an identical experience of that of D. L. Moody, as we see from his Memoirs; he was newly converted and alone in his law office when the following incident occurred in 1821:

"But as I returned and was about to take a seat by the fire, I received a mighty baptism of the Holy Ghost...the Holy Spirit descended upon me in a manner that seemed to go through me, body and soul. I could feel the impression like a wave of electricity, going through and through me. Indeed

---

[6] Ibid. p 149.

it seemed to come in waves, and waves of liquid love;--for I could not express it in any other way...these waves came over me, and over me, and over me one after the other, until I recollect I cried out, 'I shall die if these waves continue to pass over me.' I said to the Lord 'Lord, I cannot bear anymore.'"[7]

Samuel Porter Jones, before God used him in a larger capacity of national prominence and city-wide revivals, he received the same anointing of Holy Ghost power as did Finney and Moody. Each of these men were endued with a power higher for service to reach thousands with the Gospel of the Son of God—fulfilling the mandate of Acts 1:8. Here is an account of Sam Jones own experience of the fullness of the Spirit.

"One of the most thrilling experiences of his life occurred there (in Corinth, Mississippi in 1884). He had become so wearied and tired from constant preaching that one night going to church he said, 'I am so tired I cannot

---

[7] G. Dupuis and Garth M. Rosell, "Memoirs of Charles Finney" (Grand Rapids: Academie Books, 1989), pp 23-24.

stand up and preach this evening. I shall ask the people if they will allow me to sit down and talk to them.'

"Upon announcing his text, the baptism of the Holy Spirit came upon him, and when he had finished the sermon and had concluded a long altar service, he went away from the church saying, 'I feel as if I were the best rested man on earth.' That night in his room the Holy Spirit continued to bless him, until he cried out: 'This is glorious, the breezes of heaven are sweeping in upon my soul!' For ten minutes or more he didn't know the sense of fatigue as he labored day and night for the salvation of the lost."[8]

It is important to note that the baptism of the Spirit came on these three men BEFORE they mightily used of God in national prominence. Notice that immediately after Sam Jones received the baptism of Holy Ghost fire an entire town

---

[8] Laura Jones, "Life and Sayings of Sam P. Jones" (Atlanta: The Franklin Turner Company, 1907), pp 113-114.

would be brought to Christ in the town of Tuscumbia, Alabama.

In 1884 Sam Jones was in Tuscumbia, Alabama preaching four times a day where the entire town is shaken by God in revival.

"At Tuscumbia, Alabama, he held a large bush-arbor meeting. Three and four services were held daily and people came in from all parts of the county. Some of the most remarkable manifestations of the presence of God were seen in that arbor meeting...Just before the greatest manifestation of the Spirit's work, Mr. Jones had been very earnest in prayer. He was always a man who went to the throne of mercy for the anointing of service...there was a great crisis in the meeting, and he met it by a long season of prayer.

"The people had made all kinds of threats against him, so after the night service he walked out onto the second story of the porch and knelt down in a corner, the thick vines almost hiding him. He remained there until midnight, and yet no assurance of victory. The morning hours came, and he was still on his knees. He had not undressed or been asleep that night. The great audience assembled for the six o'clock (6am) service; perhaps there were twenty-five hundred present. He arose to preach, and such power came upon the people that the town was won to God."[9]

---

[9] Ibid, pp 115-116.

CHAPTER SEVEN: HOW TO OBTAIN THE FULLNESS OF THE SPIRIT

"And Billy Graham said, 'This is a turning point in my life, this will revolutionize my ministry'" (on Stephen Olford teaching him the Fullness of the Spirit).

Stephen F. Olford

One of the greatest men I have ever known and have had the privilege to work with and be trained by, was my homiletical mentor, Dr. Stephen F. Olford. I was in the very first graduating class of his school of preachers. He taught me how to preach, he taught me how to have a daily quiet time, he taught me about revival, he taught me about the Fullness of the Spirit and the Lordship of Christ. But, as vitally important as each of these events were, God used Stephen Olford to alter the very course of my entire life! Before meeting him, I was a successful businessman who was a Christian—my main focus in life then was making money and lots of it! Under Stephen Olford's anointed preaching God literally turned my life upside down and inside out! We became friends, colleagues in ministry, and I eventually would become a member of his ministry board. Dr. Olford wrote the foreword to my first book on revival: "Realities of Revival" and we co-authored a book together, "Olford on Scroggie" about his homiletical mentor, Dr. W. Graham Scroggie. Since my memorable encounter with God through Dr. Olford's preaching I am the author of over twenty-eight books on revival and Christian living and I have over 2,200 recorded sermons on SermonAudio.

I will let him relate in his own words how he came to know the Fullness of the Holy Spirit in his own life and how he preached it to others. How he influenced greatly a young Billy Graham by holing up with him for two days in a bed and breakfast in a remote part of Wales to teach him the truths of the Fullness of the Spirit. The following is an account of his own story written as a contribution for the book, "My Most Memorable Encounter with God" edited by David Enlow and published by Tyndale House, 1977 (now out of print). Here now is Stephen Olford's story of how he came to know the Fullness of the Holy Spirit:

WHEN THE SPIRIT BECAME LORD

By Stephen F. Olford

Biblical truth and personal experience have taught me that normal growth in the Christian life not only implies but involves spiritual crises. Indeed, there is a sense in which every act of obedience constitutes a crisis. And it is also true that, for a variety of reasons, some crises are more memorable than others.

My conversion on the occasion of my seventh birthday, in Angola, West Africa, was a memorable crisis. Several days before this I was on trek with my missionary parents. On the last lap of the journey, I had a frightening experience. One of the men, carrying my hammock, stumbled while crossing a narrow bridge over a fast-flowing stream. The hammock turned over, ejecting me into the air—and on my way to a watery grave. In God's providence, however, I was caught by my clothes in an overhanging tree. When eventually I was extricated, I knelt, trembling, on the nearby bank to thank God for my deliverance. I knew, even as I prayed, that I was not prepared to meet my Maker.

Shortly after this I did encounter Jesus Christ as my Lord and Savior. Something my mother said at family prayers sent me to bed troubled. At midnight I called her to my bedside and said, 'I am not ready to meet Jesus; can you tell me how?' Thank God, she did—and peace flooded my soul.

My baptism, in a damned-up pool, before hundreds of national believers, was a memorable crisis.

My restoration from a period of backsliding was a memorable crisis. In fact, this return to the Lord consummated in my call to the ministry. At this time I was back in England, studying to be an engineer. But God made it abundantly clear that His plan for life was to serve Him as a preacher—anywhere, at any time, and at any cost.

Following theological and missionary training, I was commissioned to *"the work of an evangelist"* (2 Tim. 4:5). Then came the seven years of World War II, when as an Army Scripture Reader I witnessed to thousands of men and women in the Forces, stationed or passing through Newport, Monmouthshire. Those were days of darkness, danger, and discipline, but I praise the Lord for them! Not only were souls saved and lives changed; my own faith was tested and strengthened.

Strangely, at this point in my spiritual history I became increasingly aware of a deep inner dissatisfaction. Something was missing. My soul hungered and thirsted for the presence of God and the power of His Spirit.

This awareness of need was intensified by something I saw, something I read, and something I felt. What I saw was a local movement of the Spirit in south Wales which greatly challenged me. A relatively unknown pastor-evangelist was being mightily used of God. Under his preaching supernatural things were happening which I could not dispute nor deny. The spirit of revival was abroad. All this created a yearning in my heart to see miracles take place under my own ministry of the Word.

Concurrently with this, I was encouraged to read the lives of two men who had always captivated my interest. One was an evangelist, the other a pastor. The evangelist was D. I. Moody. I discovered that there was a period in his life when he longed to be "fully consecrated" to God. Already he was an internationally known evangelist, and judging by others, he was riding high on a tide of blessing. Inwardly, however, he was hungry for more.

Two women in his church in Chicago recognized his need and started to pray for him. they told him, "You need the power of the Spirit." Then one day, in the city of New York, it happened!

Recalling this crisis, Moody says:

"I cannot describe it, I seldom refer to it; it is almost too sacred an experience to name. Paul had an experience of which he never spoke for fourteen years. I can only say that God revealed Himself to me, and I had such an experience of His love that I had to ask Him to stay his hand. I went to preaching again. *The sermons were not different; I did not present any new truths; and yet hundreds were converted. I would not now be placed back where I was before that blessed experience if you should give me all the world..."* (author's italics).[10]

---

[10] James Gilchrist Lawson, *Deeper Experiences of Famous Christians* (Anderson, In: Warner Press, 1911), pp 345-348.

Then there was the biography of F. B. Meyer. I had read most of his books and had been enriched by the instructional and devotional depths of his expositions. But once again, a specific paragraph from his story by A. Chester Mann arrested me.

It was at the Keswick Convention where F. B. Meyer "got his first glimpse of fully surrendered service, and where he yielded himself obediently to the heavenly vision. *Meyer had to acknowledge that, during the earlier years of his ministry, his service was without power with God or special favor with man. Then there came that moment when he saw the emptiness of mere service, and cried to God…to take supreme control of his life, guiding and directing…his ever plan. From that time on God ACCEPTED his service…"[11]*

In my study of these men, I was particularly impressed with the fact that their enduement with power came after years of "fruitful" service for God. I remembered how Jesus talked about "fruit," "more fruit" and "much fruit" that glorified the Father (John 15:2, 4,8).

---

[11] A. Chester Mann, *F. B. Meyer* (Old Tappan, NJ: Revell, 1929), p. 106.

Up until now, I had been content with "fruit," or possibly "more fruit"; but what I had seen and read deepened what I now felt. I wanted "much fruit" to be sure; but more than this, I want *freedom* to be and to do all that would glorify the Father. I was fettered and frustrated in my Christian service, and I longed for the liberating power of the Spirit.

This led to action. Clearing my calendar for a period of two weeks, I decided to retreat to some quiet place to read and wait upon the Lord. I made arrangements to stay at a little cottage in Porthcawl, on the south coast of Wales. I took with me two suitcases of books, including the works of Calvin and Owen on the Holy Spirit. Titles of more modern writers were *Veni Creator* by Handley C. G. Moule, *The Spirit of God* by G. Campbell Morgan, *The Ministry of the Spirit* by A. J. Gordon, *The Holy Spirit of God* by Griffith Thomas, and others.

I also scheduled a study of such portions of Scripture as John 14-16, the Acts of the Apostles, Romans Chapter 8, 1 and 2 Corinthians, Galatians, and Ephesians. Morning, noon, and night I read, meditated, and prayed. Gradually confusions were clarified and convictions were crystallized.

But theology was not enough. There was still an unspeakable desire in my soul to be set free. Then one afternoon, while reading the Epistle to the Ephesians, I observed in a new way that all the blessings of the Spirit are *already* given to us in Christ.

Paul says, *"Blessed be the God and Father of our Lord Jesus Christ, who hath blessed us with all spiritual blessings* (or all the blessings of the Spirit) *in heavenly places in Christ"* (Eph 1:3). This includes the incoming of the Spirit (1:13, 14), the indwelling of the Spirit (2:18), the enabling of the Spirit (3: 16, 17), and the uniting of the Spirit (4:3).

As I pondered these verses, I was overwhelmed with the revelation of the *divine fullness* (Eph 1:23, 3:19, 5:18) which was mine in Christ. Jesus died for my sins, rose again for my justification, and then ascended to heaven to bestow on me the "blessings of the Spirit." This I now appreciated more clearly. However, it was one thing to *appreciate* the blessings of the Spirit but quite another matter to *appropriate* them. There was still another chapter in this precious letter— and a liberating fullness awaiting me!

So I came to Ephesians 5 and verse 18, and God opened my eyes! In that familiar verse, Paul exhorts the saints at Ephesus who *already* knew incoming, the indwelling, the enabling, and the uniting of the Spirit not to be "drunk with wine, wherein is excess, but to be filled with the Spirit." It was quite obvious that here was a conscious, continuous, and conspicuous experience in the Spirit for pastors and members, husbands and wives, parents and children, servants, and masters. The question was how to know the fullness initially and then to know this fullness continually.

As I examined the text within its context and compared Scripture with Scripture, I was stuck with the sheer simplicity of it all. First, there was *the initial acceptance of the Spirit's control*—"Be filled in the Spirit and with the Spirit"

To quote Handley Moule:

"The Apostle in effect calls upon the believer to 'yield himself unto God' the Holy Spirit as to a Power and Presence already dwelling in living reality within him, but waiting, as it were, for the welcome of the soul to come forth from within and take entire possession of the whole circle and range of life."[12]

The secret to me, was the word "control." While the Holy Spirit is both contrasted and compared to wine, *He is essentially a Person, and to be filled with Him is to come under His* CONTROL.

This led me to 2 Corinthians 3:17, where Paul tells us that "the Lord is that Spirit: and where the Spirit of the Lord is, there is liberty"; or, "Where the Spirit *is Lord*, there is liberty." I had always accepted the deity of the Spirit, but I had never acknowledged His *Lordship.* I knew Jesus was Lord, and had owned that Lordship in an objective sense, *but now I saw that the Lordship of Christ could only be real TO me as the Holy Spirit was made Lord IN me. This was the crisis point in my search for freedom and fullness in my Christian life.*

Without reading further, I dropped to my knees and yielded everything to the reign and rule of the *indwelling* Spirit. No glory filled the room, no vision filled my eyes, and no tongues were uttered; but I knew, there and then, that *I was set free!* The fetters and frustrations were gone. I hadn't to wait

---

[12] Handley C. G. Moule, *Veni Creator* (Glasgow: Pickering and Inglis Ltd), p. 218.

to preach to know that I was liberated! There were tears in my eyes, but peace in my soul!

I turned to the Scripture again, only to confirm that the initial acceptance of the Spirit's control must be matched by *the continual dependence on the Spirit's control.* The verb indicated a continuous experience—"Be ye being filled with the Spirit." To maintain this fullness of the Spirit, there must be a daily repentance of sin—*"Grieve not the Holy Spirit"* (Eph 4:30), and there must be a daily obedience to Scripture, for God gives the Holy Spirit *"to them that obey him"* (Acts 5:32), and the net result is that "where the Spirit is Lord, there is liberty."

I was so caught up in the wonder of this encounter with God that I cut short my stay at Porthcawl by three days and returned to Newport to share the news! Later that week I spoke at a rally of young people in Cardiff. The large church was packed, and God moved in such power that I was there until midnight, dealing with seeking souls. There was an authority in preaching I had never known before.

The next appointment was a week of meetings at the Hildenborough Hall Conference Center, near London, under the directorship of the

British evangelist, Mr. Tom Rees. Each day I spoke on prayer in the morning, and on the Holy Spirit in the evening, and the Lord was pleased to send us "times of refreshing" from His presence.

Friday night we gathered for a period of sharing, to be followed by a concluding message. American visitors were with us on that occasion. Among them was a young man by the name of Billy Graham. As he heard the testimonies of these young people who had entered into the fullness of the Holy Spirit, and then listened to my exposition of Ephesians 5:18, he walked up to me at the close of the service, and with that resolute look in his eyes and that thrust of his jaw, asked to know more.

We were unable to talk freely at the time but made arrangements to meet in Wales. There I found that Billy was seeking for more of God with all his heart; and he felt that I could help him. For most of two days we were closeted at Pontypridd's hotel with our Bibles open, turning the pages as we studied passages and verses. The first day Billy learned more secrets of the "quiet time." The next, I expounded the fullness of the Holy Spirit in the life of a believer who is willing to bow daily and hourly to the sovereignty of Christ and to the authority of the Word. This lesson was so new to me that it cascaded out, revealing bright glimpses of the inexhaustible power of the love of God.

Billy drank it in so avidly that I scarcely realized the heights and depths that his spiritual life had reached already. At the close of the second day we prayed, like Jacob of old laying hold of God, and crying, "Lord, I will not let Thee go except Thou bless me," until we came to a place of rest and rejoicing. And Billy Graham said, "This is a turning point in my life, this will revolutionize my ministry."[13]

As I drove home that night I thanked God for the day, in a little room in Porthcawl, south Wales, where the Spirit of life in Christ Jesus made me free from the law of sin and death. I realized, of course, that I had not "attained," nor was I already "perfect"; but I also realized that I had enjoyed a *foretaste* of what will one day be "the glorious liberty of the children of God." For me, that experience was my most memorable encounter with God.

---

[13] John Pollock, *Billy Graham: The Authorized Biography* (Minneapolis: Billy Graham Evangelistic Association), pp. 38,39.

Since then I have come to see, with increasing clarity, that liberty in the Holy Spirit is not freedom to do what I want, but power to do what I ought.

This is beautifully illustrated in the life and ministry of Jesus. Prophecy becomes history when "the Holy Ghost descended in a bodily state like a dove upon him" (Luke 3:22) and in *power of that anointing* He went forth "to preach the gospel to the poor...to preach deliverance to the captives, and recovering of sight to the blind, to set at liberty them that are bruised, to preach the acceptable year of the Lord" Luke 4:18). After completing this divine mission, He made possible, through His passion and triumph, a similar ministry for all who follow in His train. So He said to His disciples, "As my Father hath sent me, even so send I you" (John 20:21), and then empowered them with the Holy Spirit to accomplish the task.

By the grace of God I am following in this train! And until Jesus comes or calls, I will preach and teach that *"where the Spirit is LORD, there is LIBERTY."* Hallelujah!"[14]

The three main verses of Scripture that impacted Dr. Olford in regard to the Fullness of the Holy Spirit are verses we need to apply to our own hearts and life in regard to this filling of the Spirit as well. These are: Galatians 5:18, Ephesians 5:18, 2 Corinthians 3:17 by God's grace let us apply them to our lives as a living reality within our lives.

---

[14] Stephen F. Olford in *My Most Memorable Encounter with God* edited by David Enlow, (Wheaton: Tyndale House Publishers, 1977), pp 147-157.

CHAPTER EIGHT: A POWER HIGHER

"May God confer unto me the same Spirit that He had given to Finney, Moody and John Wesley so that wherever I set foot on, the fires of revival will be set ablaze forevermore."

John Sung

From a study of Dr. Stephen Olford's testimony on his memorable encounter with God where the day came where he made the Spirit Lord in his life, and how that teaching transformed the ministry of a young Billy Graham is a study in itself. Notice the two young men were both *hungry for more of God*. Both Stephen Olford and Billy Graham were seeking *a deeper reality of God and His Presence and His power!*

There is a common denominator in the lives of those rare individuals who God uses in mighty ways. We get a sense of this from the heart of King David as seen in Psalm 63. David wrote this Psalm while he was either persecuted by Saul and forced to hide himself in desert places, perhaps in the forest of Hareth or the wilderness of Ziph, Maon, and Engedi, where he was hunted like a flea among rocks; or he penned it while on the run from his son Absalom, who rebelled against him, and forced David to flee from Jerusalem and enter the wilderness to hide there like a fugitive. Either way, David was in a straight. David was in a jam. David was in need of *a deeper dependence upon God and a more acute reality of the Presence of the Almighty.* We see from the following:

> *"O God, thou art my God, early will I seek thee, my soul thirsteth for thee in a dry and thirsty land, where no water is; To see thy power and thy glory, so as I have seen thee in the sanctuary"* (Psalm 63:1,2).

David is praying to God in desperate prayer for he is end at the end of himself and he is longing, yearning for *more of God.* We hear him cry out to God: "My soul followeth hard after thee" (v 8). David speaks of the cost and sacrifice of prayer: "early will I seek thee" (v. 1), "When I remember thee upon my bed, and meditate on thee in the night watches" (v6). God honors those who honor Him. God blesses those who make God first place in their daily living.

To have an encounter with God to where one's life is transformed by God is a memorable experience never forgotten and always cherished. But there comes with that "higher power" and "authority in the pulpit" and "consistency in the life" an accountability. To whom much is given much is required.

When George Whitefield and John and Charles Wesley were seeking God in times of Bible reading, fasting, and all night prayer, they and a few other Oxford students became known as "the Holy Club" for their pursuit of holiness unto God. Indeed, it is a club, if I may so speak, that has very few members. Most everyone else just stands on the sidelines and views their lives in wonder as they are instruments in the hands of a Holy God to bring forth revival and salvation to the multitudes. It is a worthy study of Stephen Olford and Billy Graham, holed up in a hotel room in South Wales pouring over the Word of God and praying desperately to the God of the Word they experienced a BREAKTHROUGH! Power and authority in the pulpit became a reality in their life as well as a consistent walk with God in lives of holiness unto Him. They each had their warts as no man is perfect but it was their *earnest desire to be used more of God* that drove these two young men to their knees crying out to God for *more of Him! More of His Presence and Power! And yes glory!*

If I may address the Lord right now in a statement: "Lord, the men You seem pleased to use are the ones who follow *hard after You*; who *long for more of You*; who by faith *go out on a limb for You*; and who are *willing to risk it all for You and "your Gospel."*

Such was John Sung, the Chinese evangelist, who turned China upside down for Christ and the Gospel in the years between the Two World Wars. Sung had an Apostolic ministry of signs and wonders; to read his life story as it is found in his journals, is to feel like one is reading the Book of Acts.

John Sung was a genius who traveled to America in the 1920's to receive an education. In three years he had earned a Ph.D. in Chemistry and turning down offers from Germany and America to enter the field of biophysics, he instead enrolled in Union Theological Seminary in New York City—a seedbed of liberal theology. It was there he while in seminary he lost his faith from the liberal professors; and it was also where he had a radical encounter with Jesus Christ and was remarkably saved with a Baptism of Holy Ghost fire. So on fire for God was John Sung, that his fellow seminary students and professors believed him to be insane and had him committed to Bloomindale Hospital for the insane. John Sung was incarcerated against his will for 193 days in that institution, and it was during this time he read through the Bible forty-four times! Learning the key word for every chapter. Sung was eventually released and returned to China where God used him in powerful revivals that shook China for God in the salvation of over 300,000 souls during his brief fifteen-year ministry. Many lame were made to walk, the blind received sight. Lepers were made whole. The power of God was upon John Sung in Apostolic fashion!

Other ministers would approach John Sung and comment on his preaching: "Your preaching is like a powder keg!" "You're sermons are like a surgeon's scalpel!" One fellow minister asked him, "Why are your sermons so powerful?" to which Sung replied, "Because of my daily repentance."

Notice when Stephen Olford described the Fullness of the Spirit he spoke of the initial filling using Eph 5:18 for the "filling of the Spirit" and Gal 5:18 to be "led of the Spirit" to give the Spirit CONTROL AS LORD. Notice also, Stephen Olford's comments about the *continual dependence upon the Spirit's control*, this was maintained by "daily repentance." But before Stephen Olford appropriated this doctrine he had to have a *longing for more of God and more power.*

John Sung read about Finney, and Moody, and Wesley having this "higher power" and he longed to have it as well. And have it he did in great abundance! This Power Higher is available to any sincere believer who hungers for *more—more of God.* It is my prayer that this little book has provided both a *challenge* and a *way* to make this your pursuit as well! May our gracious Lord continue to bless all you do for Him.

CHAPTER NINE
RECOMMENDED BOOKS ON:

THE CROSS IN THE LIFE OF A BELIEVER, THE EXCHANGED LIFE AND GOING DEEPER WITH GOD

THE DEEPER LIFE

1. F. J. Huegel, *Bone of His Bone*
2. L. E. Maxwell, *Born Crucified*
3. Stephen Olford, *Not I But Christ*
4. F. B. Meyer, *The Self Life for the Christ Life*
5. Andrew Murray, *Absolute Surrender*
6. J. Gregory Mantle, *The Way of the Cross*
7. J. Sidlow Baxter, *Going Deeper*

CHRISTIAN BIOGRAPHIES

1. *The Diary of David Brainerd*
2. *The Journal Once Lost: Life of John Sung* by Levi
3. *Life of D. L. Moody* by Will Moody
4. *Sam Jones: A New Biography* by E. A. Johnston

5. *George Whitefield the Definitive Biography in Two Volumes* by E. A. Johnston
6. *Asahel Nettleton: Revival Preacher* by E. A. Johnston
7. *A Heart Awake: The Authorized Biography of J. Sidlow Baxter* by E. A. Johnston
8. *Rolfe Barnard: Hitchhike Evangelist* by E. A. Johnston
9. *Olford on Scroggie by Stephen Olford* and E. A. Johnston

ABOUT THE AUTHOR

E. A. Johnston was born in 1955 in Oak Park, Il (same town as Ernest Hemingway). His father was an agnostic and his grandfather was a mob boss. The house he grew up in was haunted. A pastor who lived across the alley, by the name of Clem Dear, became burdened for the young teenager's soul and reached out to him: giving him his first job in his Bible book store and his first Bible and was instrumental in having the thirteen-year-old attend a revival meeting where in 1968 he came to Christ under the ministry of Canadian evangelist, Ernest W. Wakefield. Remarkably, fifty-six years later Dr. Johnston was led to a recording of that same revival meeting, and he was able to hear himself as a teenager sing along with "Nothing But The Blood" and hear again that glorious message of the Gospel of the Cross which brought him to Christ.

Becoming a successful Christian business-man (stockbroker) with a major Wall Street firm, his life was re-directed under the preaching of Dr. Stephen F. Olford, whereby he had an extraordinary encounter with God: where God called him to preach and gave him a prodigious pen ministry. The stock market crash of 2008, combined with the tragic suicide of his wife, forced him into foreclosure and bankruptcy losing all his material goods; where for a time, he and his teenage daughter were homeless.

E. A. Johnston has experienced the power of God in meetings and has witnessed church revival. He has known extraordinary experiences of God in his personal life as in the following account: he writes, "I awoke at 2am and felt like I was having a heart attack. I had been working fourteen-hour days (maintaining both a secular career and ministry) and sleeping only fours hours each night, rising at 4:30am to have my regular daily quiet time. I walked across the hall to my study and plopped down at my desk before my open Bible. And I was so exhausted and worn out physically I asked the Lord to come and get me and take me home. I was ready to go be with Him. Jesus, in the Gospels, often answered a question with a question. This was the case at 2am. A Voice (not an audible voice but a voice nonetheless) asked me the following question: "What do you do for a living? ''Investments,' I replied out loud. 'I have an investment in you, and I will receive the dividends from my investment.' Case closed. I went back to bed. That was eighteen years ago and I trust the Lord is still receiving His dividends off of me."

Dr. Johnston was trained to preach by his homiletical mentor, Dr. Stephen F. Olford and was in the first graduating class of his school of preachers. They co-wrote a book together on Dr. Olford's homiletical mentor, Dr. Graham Scroggie, entitled *"Olford On Scroggie".*

Dr. Johnston has had a prolific pen ministry with over thirty published books of some which include: The Two-Volume Definitive Biography of George Whitefield, Foreword by J. I. Packer; The Authorized Biography of J.Sidlow Baxter, Foreword by Adrian Rogers; a definitive biography on the evangelist Asahel Nettleton; a biography on Rolfe Barnard; a biography on the evangelist Samuel Porter Jones, entitled, *"Sam Jones A New Biography."* His other books can be found at Old Paths Publications and Gospel Folio Press of Canada.

Dr. Johnston has over 2,200 sermons on SermonAudio (of which about 1,000 were preached in a parking lot across the street from a gay bar). His sermons have been heard in over seventy countries and his most renown sermon: "America: Revival or Ruin" has received comments from all over the world.

E. A. Johnston is a Fellow of the Stephen Olford Institute for Biblical Preaching. He has two earned doctorates: a British endorsed Ph.D., and a D. B. S. He has been a student of revival for more than four decades and has visited many historical revival sites throughout Great Britain and America as a research scholar. Surviving a major heart attack and subsequent quadruple bypass surgery, he wears a pacemaker and defibrillator. He still preaches and writes and resides in Clearwater, Florida.

His favorite Bible verse is 2 Chronicles 16:9 and of that he states: "God is still on the lookout for a Moody who will be on the out and out for God in a life of consecration to Him."

For a list of some books by Dr. E. A. Johnston, see page 3.

Dr. S. Olford and Dr. Johnston